The Ultimate Kindle Fire HD & HDX Apps Guide

Disclaimer and Terms of Use

Effort has been made to ensure that the information in this book is accurate and complete; however, the author and the publisher do not warrant the accuracy of the information, text and graphics contained within the book due to the rapidly changing nature of science, research, known and unknown facts and the Internet. The author and the publisher do not hold any responsibility for errors, omissions or contrary interpretation of the subject matter herein. This book is presented solely for motivational and informational purposes only.

Any trademarked names that may appear in this book have been used on an editorial basis only and may not display the trademark symbol – despite this, no infringement is either intended or inferred.

Introduction

Let's face it! We have become a nation of app users. We cannot remember the last time we went and looked for information in a phone book or even had to Google something. Everything has gone to the net as well as to an application. There are applications for how you do everything these days, whether it is losing weight, finding, your true love, or shopping for something. You will hear everyone say, "There's an app for that." What that means more than ever before is that it is very important to ensure that you have all of the best options for your Kindle.

When you first grab a Kindle Fire, one of the first things you will realize is that there are SO MANY apps and options for you to choose from. The process of finding the right ones can be an overwhelming and sometimes frustrating experience. Yes, you will eventually figure it out on your own but I don't know about you… time isn't something that I can easily spare with a wife and three kids under the age of eight.

Anything that you can think of has been invented to ensure that you are able to have all of the best options for everything that you do. For that reason, this book is divided into all of the best applications that are then broken down into categories. When you have a Kindle, you want to make sure that you are getting the most out of it that you possibly can. This means that it is very important to have access to all of the best applications.

Don't be afraid to try something new, most of all of the applications are completely free! This is your field guide to ensuring that you have everything you need to be successful in your long-term trip to application stardom!

Table of Contents

SURPRISE BONUS!

Direct Links to Amazon Kindle Apps

Reading Applications

Education Applications

Entertainment Applications

Finance Applications

Cooking Applications

Games for Everyone

Keeping Fit and Healthy

Applications for Kids

Lifestyle and Hobbies

Music Applications

News and Article Applications

Unusual and Fun Applications

Creative Applications

Productivity Applications

Shopping Apps to Die For

Social Networking Applications

Sports Applications

Travel Applications

Helpful Applications

Weather Predicting Applications

Chapter I: All Reading Materials

The entire reason that the Kindle was introduced was so that you would be able to take your material with you everywhere you go. That means that it does not matter if you are on a plane or in a car, you will have access to the best material on the market. There are many new places that you want to be able to stay plugged into. That means you will have the best possible materials at the touch of your fingertips. There are many applications out there that are free, which means you will have a great amount of choice.

<u>Free Books</u>: This is an excellent application that will give you books that are on file any time that you want to access them. That means that you are able to find any genre, whenever you want. This is a great way to be plugged into everything that will keep you informed and entertained on a regular basis. Many people, however, no longer have the time to sit down and read an entire book from cover to cover and, for that reason, this is not one of the most popular applications out there. This application allows you to get around 40 free books and after that you have the ability to buy them for around $1-3 per book if you want to.

<u>Goodreads</u>: This is a great application for any reader as it allows you to get feedback from all of your friends on what they recommend reading. That means that you won't get into the middle of a book and find out that it is no good. Instead, you will be able to communicate in advance with others to determine the best books out there. You will be able to build lists based on the ideas of your friends to determine what it is that you would like to read.

<u>Wattpad Unlimited Stories</u>: Allows you to connect to many of the new up and coming authors who are sharing their items with the world for the first time. They have a library of over 10,000 books you will be able to plug into and share with others. There are also many different categories for everything you may be looking for by genre. Most of the books are from new authors so you will be learning about their talents before many others know that it is even an option. Also, you can share your books with others if you want to by uploading all of your own work.

<u>Comicats</u>: People are tired of just traditional books, and that means that there are many new ways to be able to consume content out there. Instead of having to go somewhere and find a magazine you want and carry it out, now you can have content delivered to you directly with a USB, or a DropBox account. For that reason, there are great ways to be able to consume all of the content you never had before with a Kindle. This is hands down the best paid application for Kindle comics.

<u>Rage Reader</u>: This is every kind of comic you can imagine, free and delivered to your Kindle with instant access. Rage Comics is part of Reddit and they are drawn in a hilarious style that gives you a shot to enjoy the inanities of daily life. In addition to that, there is another free excellent application called Rage Comic Maker. This will allow you to make all of the comics you want to in the same style with the help of the application. There are many great ways to be able to have access to everything that is out there and ensure that you made the right choice. You can also be creative and make your own comics that you share with others with this application.

<u>Free Kindle Books and Tips</u>: When authors are trying to get the attention of the media and an audience, they will often upload books to a website for free so that you can

preview their work and learn their style. The best thing about that is that you will be able to see all of the upcoming authors you might consider buying eventually without having to pay for it. In addition to that, there is also an excellent application called Kindle Buffet, which will also allow you to have access to everything out there without worrying about not liking something you buy.

<u>Pocket</u>: Allows you to store any content you want on the Kindle. That means that you do not need to worry about your connectivity. You will have access to all of the images, as well as the content you want at any time. You also can share this application and integrate it with many others as well, such as any social media so that you will be able to share content with friends and family.

<u>Audible</u>: A free application that allows you to consume audiobooks anywhere you go. When you are traveling in a car or are looking for a way to be entertained you will love the audiobooks because you will have access to everything that will keep you entertained. There is nothing better on a long road trip than a great audiobook. This application is the way to make sure that you are plugged in and are ready to go with great content. Audible also allows you now to use something they call Whispersync, which allows you to listen to the content as an audiobook or will allow you read it like a normal book.

<u>OverDrive Media</u>: A great new application that allows you to have access to a library of books and never have to step foot in a library. That means you will have real copy and content right away without having to worry about the push and pull of the library. There is a downloading tool that allows you to have return alerts as well so that you will never have a fine. You also have the ability to check out regular and audiobooks, for any format you are looking for.

You have the ability just as though you were at a regular library to put any books that you want to on hold so that you will be able to access them right away. There are many books out there that will keep you happy and plugged in with all of this amazing content.

Chapter II: Your Education

There are so many applications out there that keep you informed and plugged in. You will be amazed at the options that have become available within the past few years to help you continue learning. However, if you have little ones you will also be amazed at the new options that are available to also keep them plugged into all things learning and innovation. It is very easy imagine that if we had these applications as small children, our lives and paths might have been very different.

TED: Is the best possible application out there that helps by creating a great learning experience. You will be able to know more about ideas that are worth spreading. This is the entire purpose of TED. There are many things online that are less than 5 minutes that allow you to be plugged in to many of the best experts that the Internet has to offer. You will be able to find out about many of the new ideas that are out there that you might not have ever imagined.

Stack the States: There are excellent ways to be able to learn about the United States. Although this is a paid application, it is full of many excellent features such as state shapes, statistics, and all kinds of flags and other pieces of information to help you remember the facts. There are also games out there that help you to pile up all of the information, make it into a capital drop and also have fun with the games at any age.

My Homework: Allows you to be able to handle and keep all of your homework assignments. They also have a reminder option to help you as well and it allows you to have access to everything you need to work with. There is a syncing option as well, which allows you to add appointments to your calendar. Also, you will be able to have access to use the site for a small upgrade fee between any mobile device, Kindle, or a website. This is a great way to be able to stay on top of all of your responsibilities and track work when it is difficult for all parties.

<u>Study Blue</u>: These are digital flash cards that you can add text and photos to and learn along the way. That means that you also can add text and audio to the equation to ensure that you have access to all of the best options out there. You are able to sign up for a free account on the website and can use the conference as well, which is available for you to work with others so that you will have an instant online presence. And, in addition to that, you can use the camera on your phone to create different kinds of flash cards and have the best possible content you can share between mutual study partners.

<u>Speed Reading Tutor</u>: This is a great application that allows you to learn how to read faster. There are great ways to be able to learn to read out loud so that you are able to process all of the information much more quickly. There are many versions and plans of the application but with the full version you have many more options that allow you to stay on top of your learning and improve your absorption rate of information.

<u>Chamber 200</u>: This is a great way to learn new words to expand your vocabulary. This is an application that is fun, easy to use and also gives you some great details. You get all of the history and the origins of the word. Although this is a paid application, it is a great way to be able to expand your linguistic abilities. This is a great way to learn and prepare for the SAT as well as the GRE. There are also many other ways to be able to successfully learn words not to use and how not to use them.

<u>IQ Test by Webrich</u>: Have you ever wanted to know how smart you are? You will be very happy to know there are many new options out there to be able to test your

intelligence. You can choose from many features and areas to work with, such as Verbal Analogy, Numbers, Reasoning and Comprehension. In addition to this, you will be able to learn what your genius number actually is.

Language Applications by Babbel: You have the ability to learn a new language for free. There are 11 different languages that you can learn and for the best price: free. You have the ability to download parts of the full course for free. There are various ways to be able to consume this content; whether you want to listen to lessons, use automatic translation, or be a part of a chat forum these are all methods you can use to learn the language.

Speed Anatomy: You have the ability to find out everything that you have ever wanted to know about your body. You will be able to learn from flashcards that are on your Kindle. In addition to that, you will be able to see the name of the organ, as well as the spot of the body, which you have to find before you run out of time. This is a great application for children who need to learn the structure of the body.

Dictionary: This is a great application that allows you to download the entire dictionary for free. You will be able to have access to all of the words and meanings in multiple languages. One of the best parts of this application is the fact that you will be able to see everything in your language in real time and will also be able to check it in many different languages. This is one of the many options out there for you to be able to conquer all of your language needs and stay on top of everything for learning new words and new languages.

Wapedia: This is an excellent free edition of an online encyclopedia that allows you to access everything that you ever wanted to know about a particular subject. In addition to the standard features you would find in any encyclopedia, you will also be able to find all of Wiki's other resources such as their travel site and news site. Here you will be able to stay plugged in to all information and bring your contextual understanding to a whole new level.

<u>Bible by You Version</u>: This is a great application that allows you to look at every version of the Bible that you would like to see. It also allows you to start your own Bible group and ensure that you are able to spend plenty of time working on creating your own parameters. There is also a function that allows you to connect with other readers and users in real time to share information and chat about the Bible. The application is available in any language and will allow you to interact with others in whatever language you wish. This is a very powerful tool to be able to share with others.

<u>IQuran</u>: This is a free application which allows you to hear the Quran in Arabic or in English. There are also very helpful versions that allow you to learn the pronunciation of the Arabic as that version guides you through all of the steps online.

<u>Periodic Table</u>: This is an excellent online chemistry application that allows you to learn everything about the table, as well as the history of each of the elements. This is a great way to engage a new chemistry learner who really wants to be able to understand the fundamental building blocks of the entire process. By spending the time and helping them learn all of the elements in a fun and creative way, learning becomes much more of a game than a difficult experience.

Chapter III: Being Entertained

It is very important to stay entertained both when you are traveling and when you are at home. There are some great applications out there that will ensure you are entertained when you are on the go and that you have access to everything to keep you smiling. You can use your Kindle as a television when you travel. In addition to this, you also have the ability to listen to any kind of audio content that is out there, which will keep you entertained. There are many applications out there that you just have to have to keep you up on all of the latest fun options.

Movies by Flixter: This application is completely free and allows you to know of upcoming movies in advance and plan to attend their release dates. You can see what is going to be coming in the upcoming part of the year and schedule and plan out when you want to see them. You also can access everything about them from the Rotten Tomatoes plug-in, which comes from the application and has everything you need to know in it. So, if you are more of a homebody and want to wait until the movie comes out on DVD that is an option as well.

Fandango Movies, Times, and Tickets: This is a completely free application that will let you find out the movies starting this week, as well as where they are playing. If you travel a lot and do not have access to a local area theater, you will be able to find a location on your Kindle and will be able to have a ticket that you can scan when you arrive at the theater. You will be able to avoid the pain of standing in the line, and you will be able to walk straight into your movie without delay.

Netflix: As long as you have an account, you will be able to access tons of movies and television shows on the go. Recently Netflix has started producing their own television shows such as never has been done in the past. For that reason, now it is possible to sit back and relax while you are entertained and have access to all of the best shows, which are brought to you by a touch of your fingertips. You have to pay for the Netflix service but you do not have to pay for the content you are streaming. This is a great application that works with a strong Wi-Fi signal and will keep you happy and entertained.

HBO Go: This is a great way to stay on top of all of your HBO shows. There is never a guarantee when you travel that you will be able to get your shows. However, you will be delighted to know that it is now possible to get them and take them with you on the go wherever you may be heading. All you need to make sure of is that you have a subscription and then you can pause your shows and watch them anywhere, even in the car. You need to make sure you have a good Wi-Fi signal to avoid viewing issues.

CW Network: This is a free application that allows you to catch many of your favorite shows that have been produced by the CW. And there are many shows, think back to *Beverly Hills 90210*, and many more that have been around for years and you will be very pleased to note that you can download and schedule the app to be able to watch full length episodes of your favorite shows quickly and easily. In addition to this, the application, unlike many others out there on the market, is very stable and will not crash. You will be assured of great entertainment without having to worry about losing connectivity.

Podcast Republic: Since iTunes took the world by storm with the rise of the podcast, it has been difficult to find the right application that would be able to keep up with all of the content and would allow you to go back and watch and listen any time you were ready.

Thankfully that is now over; the Kindle has the ultimate free application to organize all of your favorite podcasts and ensure that you will be able to listen to them wherever you might be without worrying that you will not have access to the audio. The reason is there are now many excellent options that allow you to stay plugged in to stay on top of everything that happens with online and offline sync. Your Kindle will sync all of the new podcasts that you have subscribed to and then will let you listen to them when you are ready. This will save a lot of time and frustration as you will be able to listen to them on your own schedule and will not have to worry about them going in and out if you are in an area where there is a low Wi-Fi signal because you will have an offline way to listen to all of them.

Stick Fighter: This is an excellent free flip book animation application that allows you to create your own stick figures and create comics of them with your friends. You can have the epic battle of the century just by playing with friends and you can make their stories as simple or as fun as you can imagine. There is a free and a paid version of this application. The free version has banner ads, and the paid version has nothing other than the battle.

Scanner Radio: This is a great way to be able to listen to all of the emergency channels as they come in. Now you can listen to anything in the world. Have you ever wondered what it is like on the job for a police dispatcher or an EMS person? Now you will be able know in real time what it is that they go through on a regular basis. This is an excellent way to be able to stay plugged into all things digital.

Chapter IV: Learning About Finances

If you travel a lot or have a busy life, dealing with finances can be one of the most challenging areas of your day-to-day. First of all, there is too much paper everywhere all the time and it is also very difficult to make sure that you have access to all of the information you need when you need it. For this reason there are many things you can do to ensure that you are able to stay on top of all things financial. One of the best options is to sign up and take advantage of many of the free applications offered on your Kindle Fire. By doing this, you will be able to track when you have upcoming bills and will have an accurate picture of your finances at all times.

SpensaLite: This is a great free application that works as well as a Quicken program. You will be able to have all kinds of reports and print outs that let you know exactly where you are with your finances. You also have the ability to break things up by category. If you want to know how much you are spending in one category you will be able to know instantly. There are many ways to have access to all of your finances without having to worry about not knowing what to expect.

Checkbook: This is an excellent application that is fast and easy to use. This means that you will be able to see deductions in real time and will know what to expect the moment that anything is withdrawn. This means that you will be able to keep track of everything as it is transferred from one account to another.

Simplebudget: This is a great way to be able to remember what your budget is and to be reminded of it on a regular basis. This handles all of the information that you add into the envelopes about your particular budget. That means you will be able to know in real time what your expenditures are. You will have access to everything as divided by category, you will also be able to see what the amount is as well as how it's broken out cumulatively and the amount you are using on a regular basis.

Bills Reminder: There are many applications out there that help you manage bills. However, this is the best possible application to help you with all of the billing needs you might have. That means that you will be able to take digital photos of your bills so that you will have everything to ensure that you will be on top of all of your finances. There are many charges that you will be able to avoid by staying on top of your bills and ensuring that you are able of avoiding any late charges, as well as any other issues that might come from not staying on top of your bills.

Wikinvest Portfolio: The market is very volatile and we are always trying to find out what the next move is going to be. Nicely, this application is completely free and you will not have to wonder what is going on, nor how your investments are being handled. Instead of worrying about phoning a broker or spending time looking through countless pages, you will be able to instead stay on top of everything right away. That means that you will be able to have access to numbers in real time. In addition to that, there are other investments in 401ks and there are also many other tools that provide access to all of the numbers in real time. When you are able to stay on top of all of these numbers you will be able to know what to expect. The application also has a unique way of being able to receive an email weekly so that you will be able to know where something is in real time.

Bloomberg: This is the premiere application in all things financial. The application could have been very expensive; however, it has been made free of charge to make sure that you are able to stay on top of everything that has to do with your finances. If you are uncertain about what the market is going to do, you can predict it pretty easily by watching the trends discussed by the editors. The application also ensures real time instant updates to your Kindle, which will keep you plugged in to everything that is happening with the market. That means you will be able to know where your stocks are during the course of the day. You will also be able to keep up with your net worth, as well as all of the different indices on the market at any moment in time.

The Coupons App: This is a great way to be able to save money when you are on the go; sometimes it can be very difficult finding a way to handle coupons. The largest reason for this is that you have to cut them out and then must deal with the process of organizing them and then finding ways to use them. You can use the application and add them to the Kindle Fire itself, then the vendor is able to scan your screen and you have a green solution, which will help you save money over the long term, too. You can use the searching function of the application to check out all of the other options, which are also available to you at other stores.

Turbo Tax: This application allows you to file all of your taxes online and not have to worry about fretting over the amount of time that it takes to file your taxes, or the amount of work that goes into the process. By having a mobile application, you will be able to know what all of your information is for your taxes, as well as look at prior years of tax returns on your Kindle. One thing that also makes this extra wonderful as well is you will be able to see all of the deductions and view the entire process from start to finish. Many people fall behind when it comes to filing their taxes because they cannot work out the time table; now it is possible to handle everything quickly and efficiently online with your Kindle.

My Tax Refund by Turbo Tax: This is another excellent application that allows you to track in real time where your refund is going. If you are looking for your refund, you can log into the site and find out where your refund is and when you should be expecting it.

That also means that you will also be able to access many excellent options, which ensure that you can plan what it is that you are going to do with your refund.

Mortgage Calculator and Rates by Zillow: One thing that is very helpful if you have been thinking about buying a house as it can be very challenging because you do not know how much you should be paying, nor do you know how much you can afford. This application will help you see in real time what the rates are and how much you should be paying to ensure that you are not being taken on a ride with the rising price of rates or of a particular market. That also means that you will not need to worry about accidentally ending up upside down in a mortgage if you are planning and structuring all of your purchases correctly and watching the patterns in the market. The application also gives you the ability to be able to handle everything about your purchase from the application; you will be able to go in and find the right individual solution for you.

Pocket Diner Tip Calculator: This clever application allows you to know exactly what the tip should be with a little bit of math. It also allows you to be able to figure out what the portion of the bill is for each person at the table. This way you are able to add people to the bill; find out what the tax is; and you will be able to add a list of your friends and family in the application before you arrive. That way you will always know how much you should tip and what your responsibility is for your portion of the bill.

Chapter V: Everything Culinary

If you are a lover of food, there is no doubt that you have been looking for a few excellent applications that allow you to scope out that journey and prepare yourself for a journey that will assuredly tempt your taste buds. Here are many of the best applications available for you on the market.

Allrecipes.com Dinner Spinner: This is a free application that mirrors the website. It allows you to find any kind of theme that you are looking for, whether you are looking for something that is gluten-free, something that is Paleo, or low carb, you will be able to find it here. You will be amazed at all of the options out there, as well as all of the recipes that are submitted by different people all over the world; you will be able to find something that will look and taste great and will assuredly be the solution for what you were looking for and craving.

Pepperplate Recipe, Menu, and Cooking Planner: This is an excellent application that allows you to collect and plan many meals while you are on the go. In addition to this, you have the ability to take all of the recipes that you have in various locations and sync them to your Kindle. You will be able to access them from the local drive on your Kindle at any time without having to worry about them not being available due to the fact that you do not have any kind of Wi-Fi connection at the moment. You will finally have everything in one place and, better yet, you can share all of these items via Facebook and Twitter as well.

Food Planner: This is an excellent application that allows you to be able to save money and also eat better; since the application keeps track of everything you will be able to use this to come up with meal plans, as well as to add and create new recipes. If you are on the go, you will also be able to access everything that you need to be able to back up all the data online and plan very healthy options even while traveling. This helps to take out much of the guess work and ensures that you will have the best options for your health while you are on the road.

<u>iCooking App Series</u>: This is an excellent application that allows you to learn the basics of any kind of cooking. If you want to learn how to make sushi, you can do it instantly with the steps and photos. You will be able to learn how to make any kind of cuisine while learning all of the basics of cooking, without all of the experimentation which has been a part of that in the past.

<u>Cupcake Recipes</u>: Let's face it. Everyone loves cupcakes; if you have little ones you know this all too well. You find yourself making exotic cupcakes and not even being sure what the occasion is for the children; well no more of that. Now you will be able to learn all of the steps with this kind of baking and will be able to access many new ideas for new confectionary excellence!

<u>Knowledge Book Cooking</u>: This is an excellent application that helps you to learn how to cook relatively hassle free. That means that you will be able to learn some of the basics in your own time and know how to be able to structure your recipes. You will learn about the metric system, the standard system, as well as how to do basic things like boil water. This is a great application to help you with all of those basics that we know are not so easy. In addition to that, the application is completely free so you will be assured of excellent options, as well as also the ability to learn the skills.

<u>Andy's Egg Timer</u>: We have all made mistakes when we were boiling an egg or cooking one. This application allows you to set the timer and see how long you should be working to ensure that you do not overcook it.

<u>Urbanspoon</u>: This is a great application to help you when you are traveling and are looking for somewhere to have dinner. It can be sometimes a bit difficult when you are not able to find the right match and you are not familiar with your surroundings. You will be delighted to note that you will be able to check out all of the restaurants around you as well as their ratings. If you are in a strange city and you do not know the area, you will not be able to find the right accompaniment for your taste buds. The application is free, adds all of the pricing information, as well as the menus so that you will be able to see what to expect.

<u>Papa John's</u>: If you have ever been at a meeting late or have been in a situation where you just really needed pizza, then this is a great application for you, it is free, it will allow you to order a pizza over the application and sit back and relax while the pizza is delivered to your location. Whether you are looking for wings, breadsticks, or pizza, you will have it delivered to you right away without complication. You can create a payment profile, which can be saved for future purchases.

<u>Dominos</u>: This is another application that brings the food to you. Dominos offers competitive prices, specials when you call or order online, and many deals when you buy in bulk. Ensuring that you are able to have any options you want whether it is dessert, or something else, you will be pleased to note that Dominos has many options that will not let you go hungry. Dominos is known for being the more competitively priced of the two options mentioned here, so you will have a free application and an aggressively priced pizza.

Chapter VI: For the Little Ones, and Those at Heart Gaming and Fun

Games are something that we never get tired of and there are many great ways to make sure that during down time in the car you are never bored again. Games are one of the primary reasons why people get a Kindle Fire, and they are also one of the reasons people keep playing games. There are many kinds of games available: from role playing, to games for little ones, action adventure, and anything else you can imagine. Here are a few of the best for you to have a great time.

Where's My Water: Brought to you by the amazing minds at Disney, this is an application that will entertain you for hours. It is the story of an alligator that lives in the sewer and is always looking for a shower. And the fun thing is that Disney has continued to update this game with new levels, new music and other challenges on a regular basis. There is a free version that contains a few ads as well as a paid version that allows you to play with no advertisements. This is a great game for little children because it is Disney; you know you never need to worry about the content or who would not approve of what is contained herein.

Style Me Girl: This is a fun game for young women who love to shop and all things fashion. You are able to dress up your character and design all of the accessories. Then you would be amazed at all of the options you have to find something that is cute and then start a fashion shoot. You can share the ideas with your friends and you have the ability to work together to earn money and afford new options for your character.

Temple Run 2: Temple Run is the story of an explorer; channel your inner Indiana Jones. You must run with the idol so that you are not caught. You will have every kind of bad character chasing after you and attempting to take your idol. Only by fleeing are you able to guarantee your life and the safety of the idol. This is a great game for little kids and family members alike and it is also one of the most popular the world has ever seen with over 160 million downloads internationally already.

SushiChop: Is a fun game that allows you to learn how to cut with no dangerous implements. SushiChop is a fun interactive way to allow children to use touch screen technology. Players must work hard to create different kinds of sushi rolls and then must be able to cut and slice them to have as many different kinds of sushi as you can imagine quickly and easily. This game is completely free and is great for helping with improving hand- eye coordination. There are also some very fun Fruit Ninja and Ninja Fishing games that ensure that you have a great time increasing your dexterity with different objectives.

Angry Birds: This is a classic and free game. It is a war of pigs and birds in which they try to get closer to one another. There are many levels you can play and you can interact with friends. The game gets more fun when you think about the other incarnations of the game available, such as Angry Birds Star Wars II, which has the Angry Bird Characters with a Star Wars theme.

FIFA14: Who would not want to be in control of all of the best soccer teams in the world? FIFA has created an amazing game that allows you to do just that. That means you will be able to be in the middle of the World Cup Action in Brazil and see all of the 32 International Teams taking a shot at being the World Champion! The game is a lot of fun and allows you to have access to all of the international leagues; you also can hear the commentary in many different languages and build teams that cross leagues. This game is the official FIFA Application for experiencing the World Cup virtually, in partner with EA Games.

Jewels: This is a jewel game that will leave you spell bound. Based on the classic game, there is nothing better than seeing how much you can increase your speed. That means you will be racing against the clock and trying to improve your score while also improving your matching abilities with all of the of the jewel pairs as they fall from the top. One thing you must expect, is your sense of urgency to increase as you try to beat the clock.

Shoot Bubble Deluxe: There are many variations of the classic theme of a bubble shooting game. However, one thing that never gets old is the ability to be able to look at all of the fun effects as well as the great levels of challenge. In addition to this game, there is also another free game called Bubble Buster, which is an excellent way to be able to have access to options.

Flow Free: A great and addictive game which will keep you looking at many different routes as you find pairs of dots and then map out a connection. You connect as many of the dots of the same color as you can. Then you have many different fun images that are coming about. There is also a free application that helps you to work toward expanding your mind. If you find that you have gotten stuck for any reason, you will be able to check and determine if you want to buy hints. By buying hints you will be able to work on the process of finding your way out of the maze.

Bowling Paradise: A free, new application that allows you to play in a virtual lane against your friends and family. You will be amazed at how much you can improve your skill. You will have the ability to choose your situation in the lane, your demonstration and will be impressed with the motion of the pins and the bowling ball. The application also gives you the chance to change the spin of the ball. You will be able to improve your hand-eye coordination as well as have a fun time with up to four players.

<u>Despicable Me</u>: If you love the *Despicable Me* movies, you will be very excited to note that there is a free application that allows you to have a virtual role with the minions. The plot of the game is many of the different minions are competing to impress the boss. That means you must try to outperform your competition as well as move forward with the process of navigating through obstacle courses while having fun in the Disney universe. The graphics and the interaction are top of the line and kids really enjoy having a place in the world of the minions.

<u>Plug The Wire</u>: This is a great game that is free and allows for the players to combine ways of completing circuits and also to improve the field of play. That means that you have the ability to complete all of the levels and you will also be able to plug in and access energy. There are over 175 unique levels in the application that allows you to have a great time with all of the graphics, and all of the ways to work up through the complicated puzzles. The game has many different forms of ads as well to ensure that it is kept free.

<u>Cartoons Shadow Quiz</u>: We all remember watching our favorite cartoons as a child. You will love this game as you can take yourself back in time and experience some of the most fun times watching cartoons. The objective of the game is to identify the silhouette of the cartoon character displayed, which means some of the characters will be very retro and some will be more modern. Maybe you can play with your child as some of the options will be very difficult to determine and others will be easier to decide on. The application is completely free and fun for hours for individuals or groups of little ones.

<u>My Talking Tom</u>: Virtual pets have been on the market for many years, and if you have a child who is convincing you that they need to have a pet, this is a great way to determine if they are ready for it. My Talking Tom is a kitten who has very distinct needs: he needs to be fed, watered, loved and tucked in. That means that he needs constant attention and care. When you are away for a long period of time you will get notifications telling you that he needs some care. It is very important for you as a parent, even a virtual one to care for your kitten. You also have the ability to have parrots, and dogs from other applications, which have been made by the same developer. You can customize almost everything about the kitten including his dress, his hats, and all of his accessories. This is a fun and rewarding application and it is free.

<u>7 Little Words</u>: This is a great application that allows you to access 50 challenging word puzzles, which are similar to crosswords, but so much more fun. You will be given seven clues and twenty letter groups to mix and you may find out a way to be able to move forward with all of the challenges. There are 50 free levels, but if you want to expand and take on the next challenge you can also pick up the paid application, which will keep you on the edge of your seat and very confused.

Chess Free and Checkers Free: These are two games that we all grew up with and learned how to play as small children. However, now there are online versions that are free and allow you to play against your friends or the computer. If you think that you are a wizard at strategy, spend the time required to learn how to play chess or you can take on your friends at checkers. It is a timeless game that never grows old.

Solitaire: A classic game that never gets old. This is a game that allows you to have a great command of the game and to play with simple and fun effectiveness. You can change the design on the cards--you can use your photo as the card logo if you like. You also have the ability to customize whether the game is left-handed or right-handed in the way that the game is dealt.

<u>Enjoy Sudoku</u>: A Japanese trend that has swept the minds of mathematical thinkers for many years. Many people never get tired of the game; for many years you have seen people who are walking around sporting the books and doodling away trying to ensure that they stay ahead of others. Now you can play with others, and compete against them, in addition to having over 10,000 different puzzles. You will be able to customize the view as well as look at many different configurations that will make things much more fun for you as a Sudoku addict.

Chapter VII: Keeping Healthy

With all of the innovations out there, there is no reason why you should not be the healthiest version of yourself possible. That means that whether you are trying to lose weight, get pregnant, or lower your blood pressure you will have access to all of the best options online by making sure that you are able to use online applications to track everything. Kindle Fire has offered you some of the best options that will ensure that you are able to be healthy and also monitor many things for free.

Web MD: Sometimes you may have gone to the Web MD site and you may have seen there are many symptoms that could cause you to worry if you are not careful to make sure that you are on track. To make a long story short, this is a great application as long as you do not start diagnosing yourself. You are able to look at all of the symptoms you have and will be able to find many other symptoms and also know what you might have. There is also an excellent offline first aid demo that will help you in the event of an emergency. That means that you will be able to access the content and act smartly in a bad situation.

Medscape: This is a great application for health professionals as well as students. The application has clinical and medical information and it is free. It has tons of information on disease and conditions as well as procedures and drugs. There are also many pieces of information that assist you. In addition to this, you can see all of the drugs and minor conditions. There is also a great update that allows you to use this as an insurance plan application as well and you will be able to read all of this content offline. This is very helpful and excellent to ensure the best possible information.

<u>Epocrates</u>: This is a great application that gives you information on drugs all through the country. You can also check all of the drugs you are taking and check out the interaction of them with other items. You can check over 30 drugs at one time, and use the Pill ID feature to identify the drugs and ensure that you are on top of all of the items. The free version is excellent and if you want the paid version you will also have some extra options to access new features and a new user interface.

<u>Calorie Counter and Diet Tracker</u>: There are few other applications that are less comprehensive than this one. There are over 590,000 different items in the database and will allow you to use it and ensure that you are being as healthy as possible. There are many options to create a free application with My Fitness Pal and you will be able to create a profile that will enable you to manage everything online. There are many applications out there that help you find all of the ways to burn calories and improve your overall health. You also will be able to generate reports on your health and your progress.

<u>Lose It</u>: There is a great application which will allow you to set goals for a great weight loss plan. With this application you will have something that is easy and streamlined. You have a calorie budget to ensure that you are on top of all of your calories, as well as have all of the dishes, carbohydrates and many other items. You can post on the website and earn different rewards for your progress. The application has the ability to help you have an excellent success rate.

<u>Workout Trainer</u>: This is a great application that gives you thousands of workouts that you will be able to do step by step. You can see all of them in video, audio, and in photos. You also will get encouragement from many of the trainers who are a part of the application via video and audio. Regardless of what your goal is you will be able to

achieve it with this application that will make you an expert. You also will be able to share your routine on Facebook or with others who need this information.

C25K: This is an application that will get you from the couch to your first 5k. That means that you will get up off the couch and go from sedentary to ready to be a part of a 5k right away. This provides a great and comfortable transition time so you will be able to go from walking to running and then back and forth to ensure that you are working toward your goals. You will also have a great amount of options to have a healthier lifestyle for free.

Relax Melodies: White Noise Ambience for Meditation and Yoga. We all need to learn how to relax, and there is nothing better than managing this through an application. There are over 41 noises that you can customize what you are listening to and you will be able to listen to the mix you create over and over again. These mixes help you with meditation and yoga. They are also great to help children relax and find peace in the night. This version is free for almost all functionality but there is also an amazing application upgrade if you are not happy with all of the sounds you are hearing.

BabyCenter My Pregnancy Today: This is an excellent application that allows you to find out when and how you can get pregnant. You will be able to monitor your pregnancy on your Kindle Fire and look at the progress of your bump. You can also connect with other members of the community who will be able to share the experience with you and your friends. There is a great pregnancy checklist feature in the application that allows you to monitor everything related to doctor appointments and checkups. There is also a forum on the website for this application that allows you to share your pregnancy and your progress with others as you go along through the process.

Chapter VIII: Great Applications for Kids

Applications that are going to keep kids entertained are mission critical. When you are on a long road trip or with them on a regular basis, having something that you can put in their hands will keep them engaged and happy, so you can focus on what you need to do. Finding the right applications for kids can also be challenging because that means that the content must be appropriate and that everyone must know what is in the application to ensure that there are no issues with what is being consumed. In addition to these concerns, you want to keep the child educated and plugged in and happy with all of the content, which means that we need to ensure that everything that is picked will be helpful and will also be great for educational purposes. Why not help children to learn and also to be successful at the same time?

Sound Touch: This is a great application that is perfect for little ones who are just starting to understand technology. It has many different images associated with sound when you tap the image; it is a great way to learn colors, shapes, and animals. There are many ways that this also can help with musical instruments and allow you to have everything in totally authentic sounds and in different languages. When we were kids all we had was Speak & Spell; this is a great new revolution in learning and technology.

Free Piano: This is a great application to teach your child how to get started playing. There is a small keyboard with 13 keys, one octave, and the ability to learn concepts and tunes. The application will teach your little one some classic tunes such as Happy Birthday, Yankee Doodle, and a few more. However, the most important part of the application is the real look and feel of a keyboard that will get your child interested in music.

Write My Name ABC: This is a great application that will teach children how to begin to learn to write and draw. There are not only letters to practice; it is possible to use lower case letters, capital letters, numbers and shapes. This will ensure that you are able to teach the children in guide mode and that the children are also able to interact with the system. For beginners there is a system of stars that will give them feedback in the Kindle. This is a great free application to get little ones from the ages of 4 and above ready to learn.

Word Ball: An excellent game that becomes highly interactive and addictive for little ones. You build words by following the bouncing balls with the different words that are on them. You race against the clock as the balls will bounce and begin to disappear. You are able to watch your little ones begin to learn the fundamentals of spelling.

Card Droid Math: Math is always the subject that is the hardest to get children into, whether or not they will admit it. A great application from an early age can mean all the difference in the world to the future success of a student. This application is geared at learners who are 3 and older. They have the ability to answer a problem by tapping the answering options on the screen instead of typing; this makes things much more fun and interactive and ensures that the learner will be happy with their progress. It also has many programming options for parents that allows them to see how soon problems can be resolved. This is a great way to get kids interested in math at an early age.

AB Math Game for Kids and Grownups: This is another math application that drills all of the basics of addition, subtraction, and division. This is great for older students who want to learn in an interactive way and is recommended for students over the age of 5. There are many fun ways to have interactive content as well as find ways to make the drills harder in the application. All of the tables go up to multipliers of 12 and there are other games that can be used within the system to keep the user happy and engaged.

Veggie Tales Spotisode Collection: This is a great application to teach children about vegetables. They sing and dance and spread the good of vegetables and nutrition. They also perform a vegetable skit while they retell all kinds of tales, including Bible stories. This is also a great way to see all of the other stories out there that will be a benefit to children and spend time learning with them. The graphics are amazing, it is downloadable, and it will keep the little ones entertained for hours.

BrainPOP Featured Movie: This is a great way to be able to take in and process that learning is fun. This is a great companion application that features BrainPOP Jr. every week and gives an animated movie for little ones based on historical information, as well as fun activities, quizzes and interactive content. All the information is based on the film and weekly kids will become interested in finding more content on their favorite characters and topics. There are over 750 different topics to be explored on the application, which is perfect for little ones between the ages of 3 and 8. They will be focused and drawn in by the interactive and fun content they are studying at school in a more fun and consumable manner with this great application.

Dr. Panda's Hospital Free: This is a great application that allows children to know what it would be like to be a vet. There is no reason to send them to career day to use this one; they will be able to give injections and help all kinds of animals who are sick. There is a great interactive interface that allows children to evaluate, diagnose, and then cure the patient. There are over eight different animals that the student can help become healthy again and this application is completely free.

Chapter IX: Hobbies and Activities You Cannot Ignore

Technology has led to some pretty amazing and creative applications. The artist within you can be even more empowered. You will love some of the options out there to help you rise with positivity and inspiration and stay plugged in all day to the happy vibes of activities and hobbies you love.

Positive Thinking Quotes: This is a great application to help you remove all of the negativity in your life and circle back to all things positive. You will find yourself in a much happier and healthier place each day by starting off with one of these quotations. They will appear on your home screen and will keep you happy and also positively focused. There are many quotations from some of the best writers, philosophers, and visionaries who have ever lived.

Postagram Postcards: Have you always dreamed of making your own postcards? Then you are ready to move forward with an excellent application called Postagram Postcard. This is an application that allows you to print out an image and mail it anywhere. That means you can print out a high resolution card with a message of 140 characters and use them for just about anything. With the price of money and supplies ever rising, there is no value that can be placed on being able to handle the applications yourself. This will help you successfully implement and change everything you thought you could do and empower your creativity with your own photo or ones you can download.

XN Retro: This is a great application that allows photo sharing in a mechanism that provides you with exquisite old fashioned photos. You can add all kinds of elements to them such as tarnishing, vignettes, and many other effects. You also can adjust the brightness and the quality of the images. The application also has hidden functions that you will find as you go along so that it is very possible to access excellent functionality and you also have all of the functions of Photoshop, without the price tag.

Fire Frame: Have you ever wanted one of those nifty digital photo frames, but were not willing to pay the crazy prices for them? You will be pleased to know that now you can use a digital photo frame in the form of your Kindle. You will be able to set it up with a photo like a screen saver. You will have great crystal clear photos in which you can control the timing and the transition.

Doodlr: E-cards can get very expensive and one thing that makes that a real pain is finding the right way to be able to share your message. Now you will be pleased to note this application is completely free and you can share the e-cards that you are creating in Twitter, Facebook, or almost any other forum you want to. That means you will be able to send the right card for the right occasion and do it for the best budget: completely free!

My Horoscope: We all wonder what is going to happen to us on a daily basis. What if you could know about things before they happened? A horoscope is a great way to stay plugged in to all things that may happen in your upcoming day. If you are curious what to expect, you can enjoy this great application that allows you to see ahead and plan everything out. The horoscope application is very easy to use, easy to figure out what is going on, and excellent to work with.

<u>Prayers and Blessings Daily</u>: we all need a little motivation when we wake up in the morning. You will be very pleased to note that here is an application that will keep you ahead of the curve, as well as allow you to share all of your thoughts with others. You have access to great messages you can share with others and that will keep you focused on the good things throughout the day.

<u>Houzz Interior Design Ideas</u>: This is a great application that allows you to get a virtual blue print of what the inside or the outside of your house will look like. They are the largest online residential design firm and database. They have many photos that are available for inspiration as well. The application can help you with the process of handling a design if you need to for your project. In addition to these features, the application also offers an excellent interface that allows you to find all of the specialists in your area who can assist with any project of almost any size.

Chapter X: The Music of Your Soul

Music has a way of soothing the soul that nothing else does. When you are having a stressful day, you can sit down, listen to some great beats and feel much better about life. You will be amazed at some of the different applications that are out there that allow you to be a part of the infectious groove and really turn up the volume on anything you might want to experience. Here are a few of the applications that will keep you jamming and feeling good vibrations.

<u>Tune In Radio</u>: This is a free application that lets you hear over 50,000 radio stations from around the globe at one time. You can check out the music you want to hear by area, country, or region. You then can save all of your favorites so that you can come back and hear them again at any time you please. The application is completely free but if you upgrade, you can record all of the different choices. It is very friendly and can be streamed anywhere online.

<u>Songza</u>: This is a great application for finding almost any kind of artist you are looking for under many different categories. There is no amount of listening that will stop your service and it is completely free. There are many libraries of music that have been listed by experts and they are arranged by mood, decade, and kind. You can look for relaxation music, or workout music, or whatever will fit your fancy to ensure that you have the best choices for all of your musical needs.

Spotify: This is a free application to download and they will give you a free 30 day trial of Premium, the one thing to note is that after 30 days you must subscribe. When you subscribe you then can listen to any album anywhere and listen to everything that is on the market.

Nwplyng: This is a great way to be able to build your own personal soundtrack. Have you ever wondered what it would be like if you could create a soundtrack for your life and your friends lives online? Now you can and you can then share those songs with everyone in the social media landscape. You can share your personalized mix with all of your friends.

SoundHound: This is an excellent application that allows the system of speakers to listen to the tune you are humming, singing, or playing on the radio. The application will then listen and report back on the name of the song. This is a great way to find out the title and artist of that album that you can never remember. Or that ditty you are always singing.

Speaker Boost: Another amazing application that is completely free. It allows you to enhance the capacity of the sound and to enjoy everything about the noises you are hearing. This application is the Speaker Boost that allows you to increase your listening pleasure and ensure that you can hear something beautiful, while others are struggling to listen through headphones.

Sonic Loops: This is a great way to learn the mixing piece as well as multitrack playback all on one application that is completely free. If you have been thinking about or dreaming of becoming a DJ, this is a great way to get started--although you will not be a DJ overnight. This is a very addictive application and many people create their own dance mix and style on a regular basis. You will be able to have everything in sync and produce the best tracks that you can keep to yourself or share, depending on what your desire may be.

Mini Lyrics: If you have always wanted to be able to sing along to your favorite You Tube videos, now is the time to let out your inner diva. You will be able to choose the song you want to listen to, and then follow along with all of the lyrics; this will allow you to choose many of the most popular songs and sing along with them, even those that have just been released. You will be very pleased to note that there are many solutions out there that will keep you happy as well as plugged in to the music.

Plasma Sound: This is another great application that is completely free and will allow you to turn your Kindle Fire into an instrument. If you have dreamed of being a composer you will be ready to let your inner inspirational animal out! You will be able to find all of the different forms of the pitch and see the graphics of the pitch along the axis of the music. There is a continuous display that will paint the music for you and allow you to plan your own symphonies. This is a great way to get into music and inspire children about all of the potential applications they can plug in to.

Mobile Sheets: Being a musician can get a little messy sometimes; you are always hauling around a lot of paper and are looking to find ways to be able to carry it all over the place. Now you can see all of your music on the screen of the Kindle Fire, which will make things much easier and more organized. The application has a built in metronome as well as a pedal support that you are able to get.

You will be amazed at how easy it is to get around with all of your music without having to worry that you will not be able to access it all. There is also an excellent library that accompanies all of the content and the chords. The developer also listens to all of the suggestions that come in through the website and ensures that all of your needs are met and everything is handled on time.

Chord: This is another free application that is great for handling all of your chords; you will no longer be lugging around heavy books. You are now able to access everything that you need. You will also be able to know what any chord would sound like by listening in real time and trying the strumming function on your phone.

Chapter XI: All Kinds of Articles in Print

Remember the days before the Kindle, when you spent all of your time getting your hands very dirty and dealing with them just to be able to read the magazine. Now all of that is long in the past. There are many great ways to be able to handle all things that allow you to handle everything digitally. You want to make sure you have access to all of the best options on your Kindle. Here are the best possible applications to help you with this.

Newshog: This is a great application to ensure that you are on top of everything that is happening in this international world. In a world that just won't ever stop, it is very important to make sure that you are plugged in to all of the latest headlines. Since this application's from Google, you will be right in the middle of the best news source available right now on the Internet.

Google organizes over 100 channels to help get the content you need. You will be able to save the stories that you want to read without worrying that you won't be able to access them later on. This keeps you plugged in and let you access them at any time without worry. And of course, the application is the best price, free.

Zinio: This is an excellent application that allows you to find your favorite magazine title. You will be able to find anything that you can think of and will be able to find the different publications by category and you know you are going to have access to the read section at any time. The application also lets you know about upcoming offers and sales.

BBC News: As the world's most respected news outlet, you are always plugged in when you have this application in your pocket. The BBC is always on the forefront of the news and is one of the best sources to ensure that you always have the most recent scoop. The BBC is the oldest news entity in the world with over 23,000 members of its staff and they are known for staying on top of everything as well as being one of the first organizations to cover many of the stories out there.

Reddit is Fun: This is one of the most interesting social news websites. Registered users are able to submit articles or post ideas of their own; however, the importance of the story is then determined by the audience. That means there is a lot of competition for the space available on the site. However, many of the stories that are picked up by the site have a tendency to become viral rather quickly. The application for the phone is in short what's hot or not on the Internet at that moment in time. You will have a great idea of everything that is trending after logging in just for a few moments.

USA Today 24/7: Is an excellent application to see all of the news from across North America. This is also a great way to ensure that you consume all of the same content that you find in the paper; however, a subscription is not required. That means that you will be able to look at the application in an almost real paper like format, without the ink and the stains, or the money paid for the application. Does it get any better?

World Newspapers: This is an excellent free newspaper that allows you to see every newspaper in the world and what is going on locally there. One thing that can be difficult is finding an application which covers the entire world. However, this one will allow you to see everything from Rome, to Paris, to Miami. The application is completely free and you can see either a summary or the full article, depending on the amount of time you have.

TMZ: We all know the television show where celebrities are caught embroiled in scandal and issue after issue. This is a great way to keep up with what your favorite celebrities are doing and hear all the latest gossip and news from Hollywood. Whether or not we admit it, we are all interested in the lives of celebrities and we are all much plugged in to everything they are doing all of the time. Why not relax and enjoy a few moments with your coffee and find out about all the latest celebrity dirt.

CNET News: This is an excellent application that will keep you plugged in to everything that is happening in the technology world. If you are curious about all of the new information that is coming hot off the presses about all of the latest innovations, this is a great source. You will be amazed at everything out there that will permit you to be in the middle of all of the latest discoveries as we move into the bold new world of technology. The application is completely free and will keep you in the loop about all of the technology manufacturers and their latest releases to the entertainment of the gaming world.

Chapter XII: Novelty Applications

Some applications are just fun. And that means you can just have a great time using them. Here are some of those classic applications that will be a blast anytime you pick them up.

<u>Instant Buttons</u>: This is full of silly noises and sounds—all you have to do is press buttons to get instant effects and you will be able to enjoy them right away. There are over 230 sounds and you can find the best sound for the moment. Don't be surprised if kids become addicted to it and want to use it all the time, following you around the house with silly noises. You may also get really great at it and then follow them around as well pressing buttons. Either way, you will have a great time.

<u>Ghost Radar Detector</u>: This is another game which allows you to see if there is a ghost in the room. If there is, an alarm goes off letting you know there is a ghost. You will then be able to record that portion and be able to decide how to investigate that ghost. As we all know there are a lot of unusual phenomena in this world, and having a fun application that allows you to explore that is a great thing.

<u>The Love Calculator</u>: This is a great application that allows you to decide how much you match your intended in the mind of the stars. This allows you to see if the application will think it will work out--much like we all used to do with paper diamonds when we were young before the advent of the Internet. This is great for young girls or boys who are starting to be crazy for the opposite sex.

Crazy Fun Facts: Random trivia is always fun. Have you ever wished you had a treasure trove of those so that you would be able to take those ideas and dazzle others with your brilliance and show them everything that you could do with this kind of trivia? There is nothing better than having access to this application, which has over 20,000 novelty random facts that will assuredly keep you entertained and allow you to also have a great time waster when you are stuck in a place you need to impress.

Heads or Tails: A coin flip has been used for many things over the years and this is just continuing it but in a digital format. You now have a way to be able to make choices about the future and know what to expect. Now you can do all of that virtually!

Cool Wallpapers HD: Have you ever wanted to be able to give your laptop a different look every day of the week? You will be happy to note that with this fun application you will be able to do just that. Kick back and relax in front of a beach scape and enjoy the look, or see a thriving city, or your favorite quotation. It is a great way to keep yourself wanting to come back and work on your Kindle when it has an inviting and fun look every time. Check out some of the amazing offerings that are available for the best price of all: free!

Guess The Movie: This is a great way to stretch your brain and find out all you can about your favorite movies. This way you will have all of the trivia you can imagine and quiz your friends with it. There are many amazing things you can do as well, which are a great way to have access to all of the descriptions and you will know the movie you want to see and then will be able to use the touchscreen application to check out everything to keep you on top of all things Hollywood.

Chapter XIII: Being Creative

Photography and creativity have never had a better friend than with technology. You will be amazed to see all of the innovations that are out there with everything that you can do on a Kindle. If you are trying to bring out your own best creativity you will easily be able to do so with these unique applications that can be used for many different things. Whether you are looking for a way to make your Kindle into a camera or you want to unleash your inner artist, you will be able to find a way.

PhotoFun: This is a great paid application that allows you to snap a photo. The photo, however, has many options for you to create your own worlds and modify your surroundings in the photos. There are excellent options as well, which will permit you to make any changes and alternative reality settings you can choose. Then you can to add them to your Facebook, Twitter, or Live Journal. You can share them at any time with others and will have access to everything and can post it when you are ready.

Photography Trainer: This is a great paid application that is loadable onto your Kindle and allows you to access all of the options to learn how to take photos as though you were a professional. You will be able to improve all of your techniques so that you have skill that rivals those of professional photographers. The application, in addition to its uniqueness, is also independent of an internet connection, which means that you can use it anywhere.

Photo Transfer App: This is a great application that helps you to transfer all of your photos between devices. With so many options and differences it can be almost impossible to find a way to be able to move everything back and forth. You will be pleased to know that this is an easy application that allows you to move anything that is necessary without the need of cables. All you need to be able to accomplish this is a Wi-Fi connection. Then you will be able to move items from a Kindle to an iPhone to anywhere else.

<u>Sketch Pad</u>: If you have ever wanted to let out your inner artist, you will find a unique way to be able to express yourself. This is a very affordable application that allows you to bring out your inner artist. With the right tools, you would be amazed that you have excellent options and also will be able to improve all of your natural talents. You will be able to work on a virtual canvas, and will be able to work with cartooning and share everything with social media.

Chapter XIV: Being Ahead of the Work Curve

Productivity is extremely important to ensure that you are able to handle your job as well as manage all of your responsibilities. There are many amazing applications that help you stay on top of everything that requires your attention. There are many options, free and paid, to assure your success. Here are some of the best!

Springpad: When you are on the Internet there is never any time to take notes, nor is there any time to write things down. Springpad is an excellent application that is free and allows you to take notes, as well as organize them in a way that lets you keep all of your information. You will also have the opportunity to have a notebook with everything you need by title. There are many excellent options that help you to stay on top of everything you need to cover.

Wunderlist: This is a great application to stay on top of everything that gets to be too complicated. Life gets very frustrating when you need lists to stay on top of all of this. You will be able to have everything in this application from your task list, birthday list, to shopping and all else in between. The application has an excellent interface that allows you to remember everything that you need to. The system will send you reminders and also will make sure that you are never late to another important event.

Inkpad: This is a great way to access everything all in one place. This is a digital application that allows you to have a never ending amount of pages and then be able to move forward with everything, which is auto-saved when necessary. You also have the ability to share when emailed or texted. This keeps everything in one place and will keep you organized.

Color Notepad Notes: This is an excellent application that allows you to have a stackable interface, which can look like a post it or a check list. You then will be able to choose the look and the feel of the notes and will be able to work all of the looks into your calendar. You will be able to set up reminders and emails as well to ensure that you stay on top of your calendar.

Dropbox: This is an excellent way to be able to share documents and all kinds of information with others. You can set up all kinds of ways to keep everything out there and can also grant permission to folders. The great thing about Dropbox is that you have a large amount of storage for free, and can upgrade to have more. By being able to upload and share content on the system, you do not have to worry about all of the space requirements that are necessary to share large files.

iTranslate: This is a fantastic application that is available on Kindle Fire. You have the ability to say things into your Kindle and then will be able to have it translate the context back to you in about 50 languages. And the best thing about that is the fact that you will be able to hear the voice read back all of the content to you. Then you will also be able to learn from the application if you are in the process of trying to learn specific information. And best of all, this application is free.

Timers4Me & Stopwatch: This is an excellent application that allows you to create custom monitoring. This means you can use timers and stopwatches as well as alarm clocks to help you increase your productivity.

Sugarsync: This is a great application for sharing content with others. You will be able to share content and files with many others. You will not need to have your friends sign up for anything, nor will you need to give out your personal information. All you will need to do is download the application so you can share with others. Again this is the best possible price, free.

Clean Master: This is an application that examines all of the space on your Kindle. It allows you to see all of the content and see what needs to be changed. There are many applications out there that will result in issues with space as well as shortened battery life. That means that you need to remove many applications to stay on top of all of these potential risks.

Chapter XV: Finding Your Best Purchase Online

Shopping is a past time that is now moving more online. That means that there are many things out there to access so you can find many amazing deals and you will have everything that you need to move forward with great new purchases. Check out all of these Kindle surprises!

<u>Catalogue By TheFind</u>: This is an excellent application that brings all of the catalogues to you. Instead of having to worry and search for your favorite catalogue while you are on the road or in a place where you might not get it, hundreds are brought to your doorstep. From there, you can choose the one you want and will be able to look forward at all of them at your leisure. They all are in one location with all of your favorite stores and all of the glossy pictures in one place.

This makes it fast and easy and ensures that you will have a great time shopping. It used to be that shopping happened only one time per year, and when it did happen, everyone saved up for catalogues. One thing that is great is that you have the ability to look at all of them from your favorite stores. After doing that, you can use the "Tear and Share" function that allows you to return to them later and let you decide how you want to use those. This is a great application to plan out all of your purchases in the future.

<u>Out of Milk</u>: We all do this don't we? We head to the store and then realize that we forgot something at home. There are many applications that have been developed to help you no longer forget the items you really need at the grocery store. You will be able to save time and money when shopping so that you do not have to worry about being constantly delayed with the items you do not have in your house. There is a virtual pantry on the application that allows you to track and to see all of the items that are in

your pantry at any time. You will have access to everything you need to ensure that you are right on target with everything necessary.

Shopberry: This is a great free application that allows you to organize everything and ensure that you have a prepopulated option of items. You also have the ability to scan everything and then organize everything and share it with family, friends, or anyone else you need to share this with. There is an excellent dashboard as well that will allow you to monitor everything.

Zappos: If you love shoes this is the perfect application for you. There are many places to use this option and access to everything that you are looking for. On Kindle Fire you will be able to look at everything that is available as well as all of the other options such as clothing, shoes, homeware, and many others. This means that you will also be able to access to all of these amazing options as well.

Official eBay Application: eBay is excellent and allows you to handle, browse, sell, buy, and everything else when you are on the go. That is really helpful as you can use your scanner and barcode to stay on top of all functionality that is out there as well know everything that is going to assist you with the pricing of an item face-to-face and online. Also the application has an excellent platform that allows you to share all of your dashboards with others. That way you have access to all of your auctions.

Etsy: This is, whether we realize it or not, the new eBay; it is a website that has items of all kinds that have been made by people. Whatever you are looking for, you will be able to find it on the site. There is everything that you can imagine from shirts, to jewelry and everything in between. You will be able to relax with the best purchases in fashion and the site is known for offering the best discounts possible of anywhere found on the Internet.

Fashion Kaleidoscope: This is an application that allows you to snap photos of your favorite trends, return to them later and find ways to organize them on the models, as well as find where to purchase them in your favorite stores. You can be assured that you will be hooked on finding ways to appreciate your new found fashion bug, which will keep you entertained and always craving more. There are many great ways to enjoy this application and to plan out everything you want to do with the fashion features.

FidMe: This is an application that can help you manage all of your loyalty cards. We all know how ridiculous it can be when you have a million different cards and you cannot find them. This is one application that allows you to put all of your cards into one location. After doing that, you will then be able to return to the application at any moment and be able to use the loyalty cards you have in one place online. This is a fast way to assure you are able to reach all of the right people.

Tango Card: This is a gift card management tool application that works with Android systems. This allows you to know the balance on any gift card by simply scanning the card. That way you will never miss an expiration date or not know what to expect. It will ensure that you are ahead of the curve and that you are ready. There are also many excellent online tools that allow you to handle all of the features you want to over the Internet; when the balance is about to expire the application will email you and will turn red on your dashboard. That will ensure that you never have an issue again with your card or with not knowing how much you have left over.

Chapter XVI: Social Networking and Communication Applications

We are all about social media these days and there are many reasons why. It is more difficult now than in the past when you were going to reach out and talk to someone. You must Facebook someone sometimes to get it touch instead of just being able to call them. Ultimately it is faster and easier and guarantees a response. Many people have given up on calling altogether or have stopped answering their phones and recognize social media as the preferred means of communication. This is great for the tech savvy and keeps everyone communicating.

Flipboard: This is a great social media application that pulls everything into one place and allows you to have a customized kind of magazine that is beautiful and has a great interface. You have the ability to access everything in one place where you can customize your feed and decide what aspects you wish to keep and which ones you wish to customize. If you are a fan of a particular topic you will be able to see a customized feed on the topic.

Facebook: This is the classic social media application that started almost everything. Here you can share and connect with all of your friends. You will instantly be connected to your friends and to your space where you will be able to communicate, share pictures, videos, and other media. This will ensure that you are always plugged in to everything that your friends and family are doing at any time.

Facebook Pages: If you are handling many different Facebook pages you will now be able to handle everything from your pages application. You will be able to put in information from the application and share to all of the different pages you are managing. This is very powerful because in the past this was not the case. You had to go to each page individually. This would take a large amount of time and would be difficult and require you to go to a computer. Now it can be handled from your Kindle Fire.

Twitter: This is an application that only continues to grow in popularity and is becoming one of the most important applications. When celebrities or anyone else want to update their status these days they are all going to Twitter. That means that things that can be said quickly and easily will be shared with the world. Make sure you have a Kindle version of the application so that you will be able to continue to share with others and also inform the world of upcoming changes in your status. It is a great way to be able to tweet, follow, favorite and retweet.

All-In-One Social Media: This is an excellent social media platform that will ensure that you are able to stream content from anywhere at any time in one location. The issue with many of the formats out there is that you do not have the ability to add it in a way that will make it palatable and easy to see what is going on everywhere at one time. You have the ability to have your own hub on your Kindle Fire dashboard. From there you will be able to see everything that allows you to track and access t all things that assist with staying plugged in to everything on a regular basis. It is very important to see all of the updates from friends as well as the updates that are being posted without having to scroll through each one.

Pinterest: This is a great way to see photos from locations we all dream of going to. People are able to share and reflect on their experiences with others. You can share and pin subjects that mean something to you and share them in a way that is visible to others and will also ensure that others can have the same experience you had when you went to that site. The application also has an offline mode that means that you do not have to be connected to Wi-Fi in order to enjoy the look and feel of your situation. It will amaze you how productive you can be when you do not have to worry about being plugged in to the Internet.

<u>Pose</u>: If you are a budding fashionista you can access everything about fashion. You can share all of the outfits your friends are wearing and will be able to help them make great fashion decisions. If you see an outfit you like, you can scan the barcode, which is a part of the photo, and find out where and how you can get an outfit like that one. This is great access to all of the latest trends and that you will look fabulous.

<u>Imo Free Video Calls and Chat</u>: This is a great way to be able to catch up with everyone. You will easily be able to access every IM program in one location, which will ensure you can have video files and everything else to access all of your messengers in one place. These days we all live so fast it is almost impossible to keep up with everything. You assuredly want to have access to every messenger in one place so you do not have to worry about losing touch with anyone ever again.

Chapter XVII: Following Your Favorite Team

Sports are one of those topics you always want to stay on top of and sometimes that can be very difficult. It is very important to know where to get all of the updates so you will be plugged in to everything that has to do with your favorite sport. For that reason, you want to ensure that you can stay on top of all of the updates without having to do it with too much difficulty. You will be pleased to know that if you own a Kindle Fire, there are many options out there for you.

Team Stream: This is a great application that provides you curated content from around the Internet anywhere that you need to see it. There will be lots of information sources that allow you to access it and you decide what you want to see. By having these choices, you will be able to access all of the best options across the Internet and will have access to everything in one dashboard. You also will have the ability to have the sports, professional, domestic and many other options to follow. The application is completely free!

Yahoo! Sports: This is an excellent application that allows you to see all the scores, schedules, stars and information out there on the Kindle Fire. You will be surprised at everything that is available. You will be able to see tennis, NASCAR, Formula One racing, and everything else.

<u>College Football Scoreboard</u>: This is a great way to access all of your college team information, as well as all of the football scoreboard information. Now you do not have to look further than your application, because it gives you all of the scores and provides you all of the information on the titles and schedules. You also will be able to see all of the past records, wins, and everything else about the team. It is completely free; however, you also have the ability to have a paid version, which allows you to have access to everything out there.

<u>MLB.com at the Ballpark</u>: This is a play by play analysis of everything that happens that you might miss if you were not paying attention to a game. There is a database that is a part of the application that pertains to all of the Major League Baseball Stadiums. You will be able to have access to all of the stadiums and everything else so that you will see everything about baseball.

<u>Golf Channel Mobile</u>: This is a great way to have all of your information for news, scores, and television. This is completely up-to-date and ensures that you are able to stay plugged in to everything for the Golf Channel. You also will be able to see videos, as well as links, which give you everything you need to know about the PGA, LPGA, and the senior tours. There are also instructional guides and other information to help you improve your own game.

<u>Yahoo Fantasy Sports</u>: This is a great way to be able to handle your fantasy game on your Kindle Fire. It is very amazing to have access to all of the statistics so that you will be able to make important decisions about everything in your game. In addition to this, you will be able to decide what players you want and who you want to trade. There are

many options out there to help you find the right choices in the form of your Football Game.

Chapter XVIII: Traveling to Parts Unknown

Traveling is always a little bit unnerving, but there are many applications that can help you have a fantastic experience instead of a draining one. You will be able to have the best possible experience when you are traveling and have access to everything you need to find the best locations to live, eat and have fun.

Tripadvisor: This is a great website that enables you to access things such as flights, trips, vacations, and other ways to research your trip. You will be able to find out some of the best possible locations for everything out there. You can plan your entire trip and have access to all of the individual planning tools, forums and many other options. This is a free application that will help you with all of the best options and help you to move forward in the process of planning.

Kayak: This is one of the best possible applications to find the best rates on flights, hotels, car rentals, and more. You also can see when there are delays; in addition you will be able to get all kinds of advice on packing and access to ATMs.

Flightview: This is an excellent way to see all of the information about your flight as you will get real time updates that tell you of any changed routes and many other pieces as well. There are also many ways that you will be able to see everything such as delays, points of departure, and all flight numbers and routes. Also you have access to this so that it is completely free, but if you want to have an ad free version you will be able to get a paid version.

My Disney Experience: If you ever thought of having a perfect Disney vacation this is the application to use to plan it. This means that you will be able to look at all of the rates available for your vacation, including the attractions as you stroll through the park. You can see all of the images, all of the height and weight restrictions, and everything for FASTPASS. In addition to that, you can see all of the dining options for a great experience. You will have a great experience because you have so much information in one location.

Currency Converter: Nothing is worse than having no idea how much money you are spending in a foreign country or trying to do math on the fly. You will be very thankful to note that you no longer have to worry about that. Now you will be able to use the nice application that updates all of the content in 190 countries, as well as all of the metals. You will not have to wander inside a brick and mortar bank but instead will be able to handle everything over the application and will be able to stay on top of everything that tells you all of the rates of purchase.

Mapquest: This is a great way to ensure that you do not get lost. This is one of many ways to access directions. With this application, you will not end up in the wrong location. Mapquest will help you get from point A, to point B and will assure that you do not find yourself somewhere you should not be.

Chapter XIX: All Around Awesome Useful Applications

Some applications are just amazing and will let you do just about anything. You no longer need to be in the office, or even have one to get many things done that in the past would have been impossible. You have access to everything out there to ensure that you are able to be plugged in and the most productive you from wherever you may be.

Calculator Plus: This is an amazing application that makes your life much easier than you can ever imagine. It is one of the top-rated applications in the Amazon store and with good reason; it is free and handles almost everything you could ever need a calculator to do quickly and easily. You will be amazed at all of the functionality, as well as everything you can do to stay plugged in and ahead of the curve with the technology.

Alarm Clock Xtreme: Let's face it; we all have those moments when we cannot get up, when we wish that our alarm clock would allow for just a little more time. Those days will become easier and easier with this application. You no longer have to worry about setting an alarm because you will have one of your Kindle. You can choose many different options to wake up and customize your own snooze options.

Lookout Mobile Security: This is a great application that is able to help you keep all issues off of your Kindle Fire. Instead, you will be able to note that you have the best option to guard your Fire. Mobile hotspots and other locations are now sometimes threats that can put you in harm's way if you are not careful. This application allows you to monitor your device in real time and know if you are going to have any issues. It uses virus scanning on your device, as well as makes you GPS traceable so you have everything you need in one place to ensure your safety. In addition to this, there is a loud alarm that you can use in case your device is ever misplaced. You will have many unique ways protect your device for free.

Advanced Task Killer: There are many applications out there but there are not many that are free. This is one that will help you manage all of your applications and that won't destroy your memory. You want to make sure that you have an application running that will conserve your battery life, ensure that you have the best possible option as well to make it run faster, and scan your Kindle Fire to see if there are any issues you should know about. This is one application which will ensure and check how much memory is available as well as will adjust all of the security settings for the application and will allow you to have access that is needed and have everything in top running order.

Battery HD: This is a free application that lets you see how much battery life you use for all of your current applications. Then you will be able to know how much time you can devote to all of your activities based on your battery strength. This ensures that you do not have to worry about running out of battery in the middle of a game ever again.

Wi-Fi Analyzer: This featured application is completely free and will search for the best possible signal that you can connect to. We all know what it is like when you are looking for the best location but keep finding yourself without any means to be able to connect to the best possible signal. Well now you have an application that handles that for you and assists you with forming the best possible long-standing options.

Kids Place Parental Application: We all need to block certain things from the eyes of little ones and you will be very thankful to this application that allows you to do just that. You will be able to set things so that there is no chance of anyone happening upon some content that is not appropriate. In addition to this, you have the ability to control almost every aspect of the content that is consumed so you have not to worry about other suggestive pieces.

Chapter XX: Staying Out of Unknown Weather Situations

The weather can be the most difficult part of any day, fighting all of the unknowns when you have no idea what to expect. That means that you need access to everything so that you will be able to stay on top of the weather and know what to expect and when. With technology being as wondrous as it is these days, there is no reason to not use the applications that are available on the Kindle Fire and remove all guesswork.

Accuweather: This is an excellent application that allows you to see all of the approaching weather in real time and will keep you plugged in to all of the needs of your upcoming day. When there is going to be hazardous weather, the majority of issues that arise with that come from that is that people do not realize the issues are coming. It is very important to ensure that you have the best possible options and are viewing the weather in real time.

Weather HD: This is an excellent application that takes live weather to a whole new level and allows you to see over 2 million locations. You can see sun rises, sun sets, dew points, and every other piece of information you could want that will ensure you have everything you need for predicting the weather.

Weatherbug: This is a great desktop and Kindle application that gives you all the commercial grade weather information for the entire planet. You have real time access to everything you could need or want to know about the current situations and upcoming ones. There are forecasts for states, schools, counties, towns and anywhere else you can imaging and all for the best price….free!

Conclusion

The Kindle Fire has revolutionized the market in ways that a tablet was never that thought it could. The price is quite affordable compared to many of the other tablet and electronic readers out on the market. What this has done is put the power of a tablet in the hands of many, who before would have never been able to afford them. This ensures that everyone in the market will have access to every tool in their price point and will be able to be a part of what is becoming the application revolution.

Take your time looking at all the options and be amazed by everything that will help you and empower you to be able to move to the next level of functionality of your Fire. You thought when you bought it that it was going to be for electronic reading; little did you know it was going to become your most prized possession. Happy exploring all of the options in the store, and finding new ways to educate, entertain, and inform every part of your mind!

References

Marmarelli, T., & Ringle, M. (2011). The Reed College iPad study.

Ferguson, C. (2013). Technology Left Behind--The Kindle Fire Still Burns.*Against the Grain*, *20*(5), 38.

Cheshire, J., & Kettell, J. A. (2013). *My Kindle Fire HD*. Que.

Weber, S. (2013). *App Storm: Best Kindle Fire Apps, a Torrent of Games, Tools, and Learning Applications, Free and Paid, for Young and Old*. Stephen Weber.

www.ingramcontent.com/pod-product-compliance
Lightning Source LLC
Chambersburg PA
CBHW061014050326
40689CB00012B/2643